WAR & LOVE
LOVE & WAR

Also from New Directions by Aharon Shabtai

J'ACCUSE

WAR & LOVE
LOVE & WAR

New and Selected Poems

Aharon Shabtai

Translated by Peter Cole

A NEW DIRECTIONS BOOK

Some of these poems were first published in *The American Poetry Review, The Agni
    Review, Alligatorzine, The Manhattan Review, Evil, Eleven Eleven, The London Review
    of Books, Manoa, Modern Poetry in Translation, Modern Hebrew Literature, Pequod,* and
    Parnassus in Review, as well as in *World Beat,* ed. Eliot Weinberger (New Directions,
    2006), *Love & Selected Poems* (Sheep Meadow Press, 1997), and *J'accuse* (New Direc-
    tions, 2003). The afterword first appeared in *Hebrew Writers on Writing,* ed. Peter Cole
    (Trinity University Press, 2008).

Manufactured in the United States of America
New Directions Books are printed on acid-free paper.
First published as New Directions Paperbook NDP1184 in 2010
Published simultaneously in Canada by Penguin Books Canada Limited
Design by Erik Rieselbach

LIBRARY OF CONGRESS CATALOGING IN PUBLICATION DATA
Shabtai, Aharon.
[Poems. English. Selections]
War & love, love & war : new and selected poems / Aharon Shabtai ;
translated by Peter Cole.
    p. cm.
Includes bibliographical references and index.
ISBN 978-0-8112-1890-0 (pbk. : alk. paper)
1. Political poetry, Israeli—Translations into English. 2. Love poetry, Israeli—
Translations into English. 3. Shabtai, Aharon—Translations into English.
I. Cole, Peter, 1957– II. Title. III. Title: War and love, love and war.
PJ5054.S264A25 2010
892.4'16—dc22   2010010440

10 9 8 7 6 5 4 3 2 1

New Directions Books are published for James Laughlin
by New Directions Publishing Corporation
80 Eighth Avenue, New York 10011

CONTENTS

WAR & LOVE
LOVE & WAR

PART I
(2000—2008)

RYPIN

These creatures in helmets and khakis,
I say to myself, aren't Jews,

in the truest sense of the word. A Jew
doesn't dress himself up with weapons like jewelry,

doesn't believe in the barrel of a gun aimed at a target,
but in the thumb of the child who was shot at—

in the house through which he comes and goes,
not in the charge that blows it apart.

The coarse soul and iron fist
he scorns by nature.

He lifts his eyes not to the officer, or the soldier
with his finger on the trigger—but to justice,

and he cries out for compassion.
Therefore, he won't steal land from its people

and will not starve them in camps.
The voice calling for expulsion

is heard from the hoarse throat of the oppressor —
a sure sign that the Jew has entered a foreign country

and, like Umberto Saba, gone into hiding within his own city.
Because of voices like these, father,

at age sixteen, with your family, you fled Rypin;
now here in Rypin is your son.

HOPE

It's hopeless, you told me,
waking in the middle of the night —
the moonlight drifting
in through the curtain —
and you looked at your wife,
at her thin, whitening shoulders
and dark hair
as she was slowly breathing,
thinking again and again
of all this evil,
the loss amassed in the soured heart
day after day, for two years and more.
It was in Karmei Avdat.
I rose, you said,
and without my glasses
went out barefoot onto the gravel
to a bench we'd moved
against the shed
and sat there in my underwear,
staring out toward the hill.
Along that slope, I told you,
five million stones have been cast:
the stones will always be stones,
no good will ever come
of them or to them —
not in another two years,
and not in a hundred.

But if you shift your eyes
even a meter to the side,
you'll see a plant
with five tomatoes.
That's where you should look.
These vile people
will acquire
plane after plane
and bomb after bomb,
and more will be wounded and killed,
more be ruined and uprooted;
for this is all they're capable of,
and not tomorrow, and not forever,
will any good come
of them or to them,
for evil holds no promise
and possesses neither the life nor yield
contained in a single tomato.
When I think of this land,
love streams through my heart.
When I remember Amira and Neta,
and Rachel in her orange parka,
and not the pus of the cruel
or their barking,
and their *boom boom boom* —
but this substance,
this certain serum
that's secreted in me
and throughout the world gives rise

to building, repair, and enlightenment,
counsel and cooperation –
this is the hope
that lends me a place and ground
in which to send out a bold root
there, beyond that heap of stones
at the Mas'ha checkpoint,
at the store run by the old grocer
with the white crocheted cap
who stands by the door
with plates of *labneh*
which he takes out of the rickety fridge;
and this is the longing and yearning
to go down into the village groves
and through the breach in the barbed-wire fence,
to cross the ditch –
turning my back
to the land-grabbers' contractor
who, with his guards,
peers out from the jeep
at the burrowing bulldozer –
and like someone in Florence
climbing to the top
of Brunelleschi's Dome,
to mount that hill
and under the tree beside the tent,
to sit with Nazeeh and Riziq,
to look into Nazeeh's face
at his toenails and black sandal,

to see Riziq's cigarette —
this is hope —
and with Riziq and Nazeeh
to look out far beyond the fence,
beyond the barbarity,
toward the border of humanity.

HEBREW CULTURE

Hebrew culture resembles
two sisters
from good families
who married soldiers,
career officers—
one called Pinkie,
and the other Bogie.
Early each morning,
Pinkie and Bogie rise.
One runs around
with platoons of artillery,
sowing death
among the poor,
destroying homes
over old and young;
and the other gazes
out through a pair of binoculars,
gradually cuts
a village in half
where groves had flourished,
and turns entire cities
into concentration camps.
From a distance of ten kilometers,
nothing is heard but the sound of sprinklers.
Books are put back on the shelf
in their handsome jackets,

and the two sisters
turn to their respective recipes
and start to cook:
one makes goulash for Bogie,
and the other – pasta for Pinkie.

FOUR ROADBLOCKS

Passersby on the Ariel road
see at the entrance
to the meager path
branching off toward every village
an Israeli work of art:
a roadblock
made from a heap of dirt and stones.
So it is at Marda
and on the way to Zeita,
between Tapu'ah and Yasuf,
and beneath the bridge at Iskaka.
I brought them back
into my home,
and now before I fall asleep
I see the roadblocks
standing in front of my eyes
between the wardrobe
and the bed.
On the one from Iskaka
a wolf's carcass
has been tossed,
while the one from Zeita
is built of five
concrete cubes
coolly arranged
in a straight line
with equal spaces between them—
like the branches of our Menorah.

SHARON RESEMBLES A PERSON

Sharon resembles a person,
and the imminent peace resembles peace,
and the paper reporting with fanfare
resembles a paper,
and teachers resemble teachers,
and education — education.
From the window of bus #5
I look at people along the sidewalk,
accompanying them in my mind,
and all of it only confirms
that they resemble people —
the shoes, the falafel, the mouthful,
et cetera.
At the grocer,
with trembling fingers
I check the potatoes,
and they too, they too,
resemble potatoes.

WHAT'S SPINOZA?

The officers rub their hands together:
Here comes the War.
We're through with killing retail,
as though in a ledger;
now rivers of blood will flow.
Through pages of sky and land we'll turn
as we take out the crates of bombs.
But how will I ever pack
all that life scrambling for cover
into the narrow drawer of my heart?
How will it hold the tiles for roofs?
How will it hide all the bricks?
And what of the beds—
and each mattress
where the body leaves a dimple?
The board at the bottom of the heart will split
from the weight of the clothes in the closets,
and all the shoes whose toes I kiss.
Those shoes! The perfection of beauty!
Canoes for the soles of the feet!
And what about all of the toys
tumbling across the floors?
How will I gather the cups
from all the kitchens?
The kits for shaving and sewing?
And what of the combs?
The pianos and flutes?

How could the creaky heart contain them?
And all those albums full of pictures
and the wedding rings —
how could they ever be crammed
into that little drawer
I received from my father?
Have mercy, please, Mr. Mofaz,
let cookies rain down upon them!
Throw them Spinoza!
"No," he answers,
"Bombs, bombs, and more bombs!
What's Spinoza?"

THE MORAL SENSE

This table covered with books
won't protest if someone removes them
and in their place lays me out
and extracts my eyes through my ass.
The diligent bread knife will soon adapt
itself to sawing off my hands.
My shoes, too, accustomed to modeling
their peripatetic qualities
in making their way to the sink
or going downstairs with a garbage bag
will not blush if someone
more decisive than I am
walks over corpses wearing them.
And it won't help if I tell the table:
"You are defined as a desk,
not an instrument of torture."
And the knife won't be impressed
if I reproach it:
"You weren't meant to cut off feet!"
"What are you shouting at!?"
it would answer me
if it could. "Outside, a million people
are cheering on a murderer,
and at his command they'd go
and bring down roofs upon the heads
of a million more —
and you're concerned with a pair of shoes,

and putting the table to a test?
And you rummage about in the conscience
of a knife in the kitchen?
I have no moral sense.
But I can assure you—
my wooden handle is fastened tight,
my blade's teeth are sharpened,
and my steel will not rust!"

THE REASON TO LIVE HERE

This country is turning into the private estate of twenty families.

Look at its fattened political arm, at the thick neck of its bloated
    bureaucracy:
these are the officers of Samaria.

There's no need to consult the oracle:
What the capitalist swine leaves behind, the nationalist hyena shreds with
    its teeth.

When the Governor of the Bank of Israel raises the interest rate by half a
    percent,
the rich are provided with backyard pools by the poor.

The soldier at the outpost protects the usurers, who'll put a lien on his
    home
when he's laid off from the privatized factory and falls behind on his
    mortgage payments.

The pure words I suckled from my mother's breasts: Man, Child, Justice,
    Mercy, and so on,
are dispossessed before our eyes, imprisoned in ghettos, murdered at
    checkpoints.

And yet, there's still good reason to stay on and live here—
to hide the surviving words in the kitchen, in the basement, or the
    bathroom.

The prophet Melampus saved twin orphaned snakes from the hands
    of his slaves:
they slithered toward his bed while he slept, then licked the auricles
    of his ears.
When he woke with a fright, he found he could follow the speech of
    birds —

so Hebrew delivered will lick the walls of our hearts.

CULTURE

The mark of Cain won't sprout
from a soldier who shoots
at the head of a child
on a knoll by the fence
around a refugee camp —
for beneath his helmet,
conceptually speaking,
his head is made of cardboard.
On the other hand,
the officer has read *The Rebel*;
his head is enlightened,
and so he does not believe
in the mark of Cain.
He's spent time in museums,
and when he aims
his rifle at a boy
as an ambassador of Culture,
he updates and recycles
Goya's etchings
and *Guernica*.

TO MY FRIEND

Apuleius, in the *Golden Ass,* writes of times like these:
A man with the head of a pig becomes king;
people mutter gibberish and turn into wolves.
Beautiful women fornicate with apes.
Rabbis shoot pistols, affix mezuzahs to a whorehouse.
Crowds drink down a rat's jokes, the hyena's howl.
New breasts are bought on the open market, one's buttocks are lifted.
The rich man farts and the nation stirs with excitement.
On the street, people wave flags made of money.
A journalist's tongue sticks out of his ass, and suddenly he's become a
    thinker.
Competitions are held between liars, ass-kissers, soldiers, and crooks.
To the sound of applause, and in front of the camera, entire villages
    are razed.
A fat man swallows a hundred thin men in public.
Thievery's adopted as the national faith, vineyards are plundered, and
    wells.
And everywhere there roams the officer, jailer, tax collector, informer.
Ships full of slaves anchor at port.
The hangman sits at the head of the table, surrounded by an entourage
    of professors.
A secret policeman is the day's astrologer, the Bank's Governor be-
    comes our alchemist.
But all these delusions disappear in an instant; a few days of rain is
    enough,
and the idols of authority, the monsters of weaponry, the masks — all
    are down in the mud.

Men remove their ape suits and wolf skins, and get back to work.

And we, too, my friend: for your grandfather and mine didn't live on
blood.

For a thousand years, and a thousand more, we broke our bread with the
poor of the earth.

Come — let's saddle our donkeys; let's go back and bake this bread:

you — for the honest men of Izmir, and I — for the diligent Alexandrians.

ELECTIONS: ISRAEL, 2001

I'm for Peepee,
long live Peepee!
Peepee's mission is civilized,
cultured, salubrious.
Peepee makes sure
the blood flows smoothly —
cleanly, and for a good reason.
Therefore, thanks to Peepee,
words give off a pleasant scent.
Not for nothing do the
leading writers and professors
express their support for Peepee.

I'm for Caca.
Caca resembles
earth that swallows
the choice words
stuck to the brow
of every
terminated target.
Caca does
what Peepee does,
but — with greater boldness,
without hiding

behind professors.
The truth in fact stinks,
but it's beautiful in its solid state.
Therefore, I'm for Caca.
Long live Caca!

PASSOVER

Instead of scalding
your pots and plates,
take steel wool
to your hearts:
You read the Haggadah
like swine, which
if put before a table
would forage about in the bowl
for parsley and dumplings.
Passover, however,
is stronger than you are.
Go outside and see:
the slaves are rising up,
a brave soul
is burying its oppressor
beneath the sand.
Here is your cruel,
stupid Pharaoh,
dispatching his troops
with their chariots of war,
and here is the Sea of Freedom,
which swallows them.

OUR LAND

I remember how,
in 1946, hand in hand
we went out into the field
at the edge of Frishman Street
to learn about Autumn.
Under the rays of the sun
slanting through the October clouds
a *fallah* was cutting a furrow
with a wooden plough.
His friend wore a *jallabiya*
gathered up to his knees
as he crouched on a knoll.
Soon we will all
meet in the Tel Aviv below—
Weinstein the milkman,
and Haim the iceman,
Solganik
and the staff at the dry-goods co-op:
Hannah and Frieda and Tzitron;
and the one-armed man
from the clothing store
at the corner
near Café Ditza;
Dr. Levova
and Nurse Krasnova;
the gentle
Dr. Gottlieb.

And we'll meet Stoller
the butcher,
and his son Baruch;
and Muzikant the barber,
and Lauterbach, the librarian;
and the pretty dark-skinned lady
from the Hahn Restaurant.
And we'll meet the street-sweeper
Mr. Yaretzky,
whose widow had hanging
in her hallway
the parable-painting
showing the stages of life.
For these *fallahin* as well,
and also for the children of the village of Sumel,
who herded goats
on Frug Street,
the heart will make room
like a table
opening its wings.
For we belong
to a single body—
Arabs and Jews.
Tel Aviv and Tulkarem,
Haifa and Ramallah—
what *are* they
if not a single pair of shoulders,
twin breasts?
We quarreled

like the body parts of the man
who brought the milk of the lionness
down from the mountains
in the legend told by Bialik.
Through the cracks in the earth,
we'll look up at you then;
under your feet
our land is being harrowed
with chains of steel,
and above your heads there is no sky
like a light-blue shirt—
but only the broad buttocks of the murderer.

AS WE WERE MARCHING

Two days ago in Rafi'ah
nine Arabs were killed,
yesterday six
were killed in Hebron,
and today — just two.
Last year
as we were marching
from Shenkin Street,
a man on a motorcycle
shouted toward us:
"Death to the Arabs!"
At the corner of Labor
opposite the Bezalel Market,
next to Braun's
butcher shop,
and at the corner of Bograshov:
"Death to the Arabs!"
For a full year
this poem was lying
on the sidewalk
along King George Street,
and today
I lift it up and compose
its final line:
"*Life* to the Arabs!"

PLEASE

If our memory matters at all to you,
please, please, for the space
of a single year or more,
for ten years or twenty,
let it rest in a little oblivion
so that it might be draped
in the pure curtain of silence.
For fish in ponds as well
when it comes to water require freshness.
And you've pushed and pulled us
to the point of utter exhaustion.
Please, spare us at least for a little while
the hot air of your pronouncements.
Nationalist blather isn't
kindly received
at the threshold of heaven.
For heaven's gates are open
and generous to all mankind,
and neither rabbis nor officers
nor those in positions of power
hold any sway over us there.
So shut up and let us hear on high
the sorrows of the Bedouin too.
The Filipina worker's weeping,
what the hungry
Indian in Bolivia's saying,
what song it is they're singing

on the Euphrates' banks.
If you've learned a thing from looking
at the mounds of our eyeglasses,
please take into account
the eyes of a boy of nine,
instead of making your pilgrimage
to the barbed-wire fences
where we were sent for extermination.
Because — enclosures intended for people,
so experience teaches,
give rise to infectious disease.

2004

for Tali Fahima

It was a bad year.
People got used to lies
as though to bread.
Toss them
for the umpteenth time
the same old fabrication
and they'll race to gobble it up
like a pack of ducks.
The stupid cruelty
pats itself on the back,
and looks, smiling, into the camera.
At the nursery they're selling orchids,
while within a bark's distance
millions of people are caged like beasts.
A young woman from the country's poor,
a certain courageous swallow,
let the voice of conscience be heard
within the kingdom of baseness,
but the fist of power
grabbed her, too, by the hair,
and threw her into jail.

BEN GURION AIRPORT

Lord Lord Lord Lord Lord Lord Lord Lord Lord
What a what a what a what a what a what a what a what a
corridor corridor corridor corridor corridor corridor
of marble marble marble marble marble marble marble
stone stone stone stone stone stone stone stone stone
and glass glass glass glass glass glass glass glass glass
so high high high high high high high high high
and empty empty empty empty empty empty empty
on the way the way the way the way the way the way
toward toward toward toward toward toward toward
the suitcases suitcases suitcases suitcases suitcases

FAILURE

1
I pray
for the failure
of this

stinking war

spread your wings
and come, merciful failure,
come

(16 July 2006)

2
Planes
rattle
toward Lebanon

diving
toward Ba'albek

to destroy
a bottle factory

3
I pray
that the plane

with a bomb in its belly

will be beaten
by the building's ceiling

4
In the name of the beautiful
books I've read —

in the name of the kisses
I've kissed —

may the army be thwarted

5
The Gauleiter
of Lebanon

has already promised
to establish

military rule

6
When the tanks

reach the Litani River

grenades will be thrown
at them from the Ebro's banks

7
In this war
I'm for
the villages

for the mosques

8
In this war

I'm for
the Shi'ite family

for Tyre

9
for the mother
the grandfather

for the eight
kids in the minivan

for the white
silk kerchief

10
Ruff ruff ruff
ruff ruff ruff

barks Olmert

11
Ruff ruff ruff
ruff ruff ruff

barks Ramon

12
The odor of failure
wafts from the mouth

the stink
of war from the tongue

13
Israel is strong

the sign shouts
from the newspaper building

spurring the diners
on toward Chimichanga.

2006

Many books,
many collections of poems,
were printed in 2006
and set out on tables
during National Book Week.
I leaf through a few,
and on every page,
from page 1
to page 30,
to page 80
and 308,
I see only
a single sentence:
Mothers and children
in Gaza are searching
for food in heaps of trash.

THEY WANT PEACE

They want peace, but they've lost their desire like a pair of glasses,
like a soft lens that fell by the sink and which they step on
because they think it's on the shelf, beneath the mirror
beside the deodorant. They want it, but their wanting is like a prick
that won't get hard, though they sit at the edge of the tub
and stroke it all week long. Their solution's in gobbling down chocolate
because they've got an appetite, but they don't know what wanting is,
what desire born of thought and freedom means – meaning it in every
    muscle,
with a will that bulges in one's pants. They say "want" –
but the word is just like the others, haunted and hiding,
and in fact, they're running and hiding from them. They get down
off the edge of the tub and try to take cover in the closet.
Each one settles into a box and dresses up as a voter, prime minister,
officer, security analyst, or commentator – stuffed pundits on tv.
You see boxes in boxes in boxes. They want peace, but they're hiding
from wanting, hiding from having to know. They're only
used to porno, to nakedness filmed on glossy stock.
They do not know what peace is, how peace is made actual and entered:
gently, with dignity, trembling, with pleasure. Every week they're
    brought
piles of rotten apples, and they lift their heads from the boxes
and trumpet peace. But it's always the same worm-eaten apples,
and peace is repulsive and stinks. They have to hold their noses.
They want peace, but have no desire, and take no joy with others,
and know only hunger. For years they've been offered garbage,
and now they won't be cheated. They're demanding actual nourishment,

big game, and not with a hunting rifle. With explosives and cannons
and choppers. So that there'll be plenty of meat — in the belly, the freezer,
and the basement. They're living in boxes, and so the whole region
has to be fenced in. They're forcing the Arabs, by the thousands, into cages
like chickens. They want peace and peace is a thing to be eaten, a feast.
They'll cut off the Arabs' beaks, and let them grow coxcombs.
Peace will drive the economy, and provide them with heaps of meat,
for export as well, and fill their baskets with lots and lots of eggs.

GAZA: TWO POEMS

I.   JANUARY 25, 2008

This minister of defense,
these pilots and these tanks

would, without any hesitation,
also kill Jean-Jacques Rousseau,

bomb
Voltaire's home,

and cut off the legs
of García Lorca.

II. DECEMBER 28, 2008

Spinoza tossed a fly
into the spider's web
and laughed with pleasure at the sight
of the spider devouring the fly —
for death comes from without
and with a perfection that nature grants
to creatures lacking intellection.
Whereas I see
the man-spider sitting in his plane,
bombarding the people-
flies trapped below —
and do not laugh
at the sight of death emerging
from within
the people-spiders
and the people-flies
caught in a single web
out of desire, necessity,
blindness, or clarity.
And those who are spiders today
tomorrow will be flies.

THE WALL

The wall —
winding for miles
between the orchards
like a pickpocket's hand —
is set deep in the mind,
and so the face
shrivels as though
between pincers
to the size of a piece
of notepaper.
Where, O face,
is your Africa now?
Where are the birds of humanity?
Give me at least two hundred and fifty
acres of average justice
and I'll find you a face
that isn't simply equipment
for searching out and chewing.

It isn't the hand of God that opens
and locks a gate
before a woman or a mule with scars —
but a stupid soldier
in scarecrow fatigues.
The wall is education —
soup kitchens
with bowls of ignorance.

And the wall is speech,
the Hebrew language,
rolling around like the wash
with which a decent person
wouldn't wipe his nose.
And the wall is rows of homes,
in which a vile man
who settled himself on a throne
rumbles from the screen
to drown out the cries of the beaten
bubbling up from the tiles and floors.
And the wall is economics —
transporting a mother toward penury,
carting the letter containing
an order for eviction
toward the kitchen table,
and driving the schoolboy who sets
his book bag down and shoots himself.

I open the refrigerator door
and see a weeping roll,
see a piece of bleeding cheese,
a radish forced to sprout
by shocks from wires
and blows from fists.
The meat on its plate
tells of placentas
cast aside by roadblocks.

I went to a village
where the hens lay
eggs of stone,
where the bread is baked
from ground homes,
and the eyes of people
peer out from behind their teeth.
Where only the mouse knows freedom.

I lift my eyes to the hills
and what do I see?
Cube after cube of evil,
clear-cut evil, spelled out
in the square letters of Scripture
with marks for cantillation:
word adheres to word
by means of iniquity's mortar.
The foundations cling to plunder,
the walls to pillars of dispossession,
the doors are planks of oppression,
and, glazed with panes of malice,
the windows hang by thievery's hinges
as rooftops curse the sky.

EDUCATION

Education needs to encourage
feeling

in a notebook one should read
and write of love

but not ignore
sloth and negative feelings

one has to study
every fact
with a detachment that really exists

a number's marvelous
in numbers there's great possibility

a marvelous compass
a compass of wood and a smaller
compass of tin

the blackboard's a marvel
smooth and square a black slate
a green slate
marvelous chalk

marvelous writing utensils
a pencil, a pen

electricity inside the classroom
is turned on only in winter

water's outside

only the lab
has water inside it

in first grade
one learns to write
writing in pencil
one learns to add

one talks and sings of the seasons
of the different
kinds of rain

for the first time in an active way a person encounters a book

and one learns to spell
the names of certain important pieces of furniture
a desk, a chair,
the spelling of pronouns,
of certain positions

one learns how to use the Hebrew vowels

one learns division

there's a risk involved in spelling
aggression inside the word
vetch
fear in the words
division, Arab

I learned
about transportation

I learned about Tel Aviv

the Bible's fantastic
especially fantastic from a distance
that's real

an elderly teacher
from Dnepropetrovsk
taught us the Bible

a teacher who always
had eczema
on her hands

I'm using
a secular language

I love what's alive
and what's actual
I love activity

I love the word *industry*

I love
the words
agriculture, agricultural

I studied literature
and poetry
I studied history

Down below,
half a mile or so from the classroom
the *Altalena* was shelled
during a lesson

and we lay on the floor
listening
to the shooting

the school had no
psychologist
a doctor came
to give us shots
a nurse
saw to hygiene

true hygiene comes
only with self-awareness

the nurse
was Dov Sadan's
sister-in-law

the school had a regular dentist

a cleaning woman
lived in a structure beside
the basketball court

the school had an office

science is studied
in the garden and lab

in the lower grades one's taught to rake

I saw
a wooden plow
one discusses
horse manure and chicken shit

on the kibbutz one hunts for a buzzard

in the field one finds a swamp cat

one shoots at a bird
from within a boat on the fish pond

every class has a house of its own

in each house there are
six rooms
and each room
has four beds

the closet has compartments
and a shelf for every child

at the end of the hall there's a classroom
at the other end are the toilets and showers

there's also a bathroom just for the counselor

above each towel
there's a label for names

extra clothes
are kept in the basement

there's another common storeroom for bikes

a shack where bedspreads are woven

the dining room's a larger shack
imported from Sweden or Germany

the students get seedlings of buffalo grass

the students get chemicals

the students get a fetus preserved in formaldehyde

the students are given a room for taxidermy

the students are given a painted sink
plugged with stencils
the students are given drafting boards

the students are given a steel stylus

the students are given a scraper

the students are given acid, oxygen, headphones

a radio crystal, a magnet, a shovel, a syringe

a hunting rifle
a trap, a sack, and glue

a jar, paint, a typewriter

athletic equipment is scattered around in the grove

some of it's kept in a crate:

ropes, nets, a shot-put,

a field-hockey ball

athletic equipment
is strewn beneath the beds

the expensive equipment is ruined in the rain
the pommel-horse leather is sensitive to dampness

in the institute
a beam is called *senaada*

from beams they built
an obstacle course
for pre-army training

in the woods
are nettles and tin

a camel foal
was raised and killed by poison there

children keep cages and pets

an older girl, Clara, became
a drill instructor

a child's in charge
of the hives
and runs the well

the caretaker's helped
by a teacher-driver

dress is involved
in education—
value's implied by fabric

inferior work
is cause for a fight

the concept of help is developed

in neighborliness
the question of hygiene arises

the margins of feeling are given
over to politics

a library encourages precision

a library drives us
to play, the body

effort in a book is arousing—

reading's work

work wounds

thirst is formed, fatigue created

the body grows handsome

on the blackboard the teacher has drawn

a testicle

the teacher displays

several means of prevention

love is nourished by giving

FROM *BEGIN*

in Brisk. She was murdered there by the Nazis. Only half a dozen men knew about the birth of my daughter Chassyah – it was one of our better-kept secrets. Life in the underground is extremely demanding. It doesn't allow one to share in the grief of mourners or to rejoice with those who have reason to rejoice. All that was changed by my daughter. The British, who'd been searching for my wife for years in order to get to me, were looking for "a woman with a child." Now there was a woman with two children. This thoroughly confused them. Where was the woman with the child? They soon lost the trail.

Chassik was born "doubly illegal." I wasn't able to give her my real name, and I couldn't even lend her the name I'd taken on. At the hospital no one was supposed to know that there was such a "Sassover," and that he lived on Yehoshua Ben Nun Street. As the rabbis say: he that increases knowledge increases sorrow. Nor was I able to go to the hospital to see my daughter. My dear friend, my soul's brother, Yisrael Epstein, took this difficult task upon himself. He lent his name to my wife and my daughter. The situation was tricky, however, and could easily have led to serious confusion. At the same hospital, at the same time, it turned out that a son had been born to a woman whose name was also (or really) Epstein, and when Yisrael came to the hospital the beaming nurse approached him and said:

– *Mazel tov, mazel tov*, Mr. Epstein, your wife has given birth to a baby boy.

The behavior of this happy "father" surely must have seemed odd to the good nurse. Instead of asking to see his wife and son, he turned on his heels and ran to report the news – that he had a son. Good Yisrael! Afterwards the misunderstanding was cleared up. We were happy. Very very happy. The celebration of the "*bris*," needless to say, would have been too complicated for the overjoyed members of the underground.

But a daughter of Israel deserves a celebration as well. Could a Jew like me, who had the good fortune to be blessed with a daughter, not offer at least a Kiddush to the congregation? Obviously a Kiddush was called for. My "position" demanded it, it was "obligatory." Therefore, we arranged for a full celebration. On Shabbat I went up to read from the Torah, and the good beadle read the blessing in a lilting voice – *And her name in Israel shall be called* ....

– Chassyah bat Yisrael (Chassyah the daughter of Israel)!

– *Mazel tov! Mazel tov*, Mr. Sassover – the Jews said to me, warmly shaking my hand.

– *Mazel tov, mazel tov*, Rav Yisrael – said the elderly Rav Simcha. Jewish pleasure filled the small synagogue. And pleasure filled my heart. How grateful I was to the good Jews who had shared in my joy during the time of my seclusion. I stood there, at once moved and a little embarrassed.

The morning prayers concluded, and the Kiddush was held. Everything had been taken care of. Thanks to the loyal members of the underground, we even had pieces of herring with toothpicks stuck through them. The under-

BEGIN (part ii)

1
Listen

to what
Begin says

The sum total
of Begin —

2
all this Begin

is
on one leg

(in short)
the *love of Israel*

3
And the inverse is:

Everyone has

his Begin —

4
Verfluchte Jude

and it's easier

and more respectable
to say, instead: "Begin"

5
So,
Begin says —

to the woman,
to the man —

Bear a child

6
Because
the love of Israel

doesn't mean
to wrap one's arms

around
some abstract neck

7
some
love on high,
immaculate
   (which yields

of course
in the end
   a cesspool
full of hate)

8
or
the sorts of love

a type like Buber
knows —

whose interlocutor
is a horse

9
Begin says

   Love

at least
your son

10
and if you love
someone

   you'll also have

to love something

11
Start with that

   and this will be

(for you)
a Door of Hope

12
But to love

is the teaching
   (the Torah)

and calls for thought
and for feeling

13
and requires
an understanding
   heart

in order to learn:

to be patient,
to be stubborn

14
To be a Jew
(as I

understand the notion)

means
to throw yourself
    into the mud

(in order to learn)

15
to learn
and learn and learn

    and in the broadest

and most basic sense

16
to enter,
really to go

up
your own ass

in order to learn
(to be a person)

17
and not necessarily
some professor

but like Jacob

who knows how to cook
a good stew

18
or like a brave
        midwife —

what'd they call them
(those women)?

hayot (givers of life)!

I seem to remember

19
And Rabbi Akiva
snuck

into the privy

trailing
Rabbi Joshua

20
and learned
three important things:

which way one faces,

how to crap

and also how to wipe

21
"That's *torah*
       (teaching) –
and I need to learn"

was his answer

(to Ben Azzai)

22
And this is the gist
of our culture,

and Rav Cahana

went
even further

23
and when Rav
lay with his wife

              he snuck in

and hid beneath
the bed

24
and even shouted
out in protest

    (when he heard

his teacher groan
with pleasure) –

25
along the lines of:

"What –
has it been that long
since you've eaten?!"

(that you've got such
an appetite)

and he (Rav)
was somewhat startled —

26
"*Cahana,
     hakha aht?!*

          Pok,

*delav
orah ara*'"

27
(I.e., What
are you doing here?

          Scram!)

And he replied
(that student did) —

28
"That's *torah*
          (teaching) —
and I need to learn"

word for word
like Rabbi Akiva

and we'd do well
to keep this in mind

29
That, then,
is what the Torah is

and Begin serves

(us)

as Rav Aba

30
and better still,
let's say, as Amram
(Moses' father)

because
these are days
of darkness
          and bondage

31
"In Brisk,"
he says,

          and (this)

Brisk
is full of risk

32
The covenant (the *bris*),
as it were,

became Brisk,

which is to say

the *bris* was crushed

33
"was murdered"
it says, and

on the other hand

he says: "her birth"
(and there's a connection)

34
"The birth of my daughter
Chassyah"

and this
    as a reminder

to "take your only son"

35
and he himself
    is well aware
(on page 179)

of what Chassyah

means
and glosses:

"*chessed Yah*"
(the grace of God)

36
And this is why
Amram's mentioned—

Say Mosheh (Moses)

then turn it around:

haShem (The Name)

37
Mosheh
is Chassyah—

    the newborn

and we will not
give in

38
Never,
we won't give up

that

Chassyah
which is Mosheh

39
And instead of "the
forgetting of Being"
(as the German
philosopher put it)

   one should say

"forgetting
the one just born"

40
And this
(forgetting the one
just born)

is therefore

the MetaNazi principle
(then and forever)

41
This
"cast him into the Nile"

      meaning

an entire world
of Ersatz

42
Ersatz, meaning
    substitution—

    that same

bottle
you stick
    into his mouth

43
as a substitute
for yourself—

but it follows

that behind this bottle

the infant too
has been replaced

44
(and for a lifetime)
   they took (as
in the story)

the baby

and put him in

the crib of one who died

45
and therefore
all of Israel's wisdom

in a nutshell

is

the wisdom of the breast (*haShad*)

46
The Name (Mosheh)
   means

Shaddai (Almighty)

and so
in the end
we've drawn a circle

around

Chassyah

47
"Chassyah was born"
   (it says)

and birth
always
  as we know

involves what's been concealed

48
"Was born" as he put it

"doubly
        illegal"

and indeed it's written—

"and she concealed him"

49
The whole business
    of this Hebraism

is
what's concealed —

to lend
an ear to what's been born

50
And "the Hebrew midwives"

(to whom
the king of Egypt speaks)

are in fact
the Hebrew that gives birth

51
And what's concealed
    in birth
(the word "birth," *laydah*)?

we ask

although
this is a question
    a fool would pose

52
The Lord is
concealed in birth —

(I say, not
without being

aware of it sounding

as though I'd just

laid a fart)

53
Which is to say —

first of all

        that *Yah*

whose meaning lies
in addition

54
the birth within

I call it

And the Mekhilta
writer's example
is:

55
The *yod* (the "y")
Yehoshua gained

    or the *hey* (the "h")
Avram and Sarai took on

when they were opened
    to The Name

56
and were given
    birth
in other words,
were given a name

and the Name (*haShem*)
is what's There (*haSham*)

57
"Invisible
    (in his action)

like the soul"

it says
(in the Midrash
    on the Life of Sarah)

58
Except that its
revelation

(in that same
    being concealed)

is also in
the letters "y" and "d"
    (*yod* and *dalet*)

59
That same strong
    hand (the *yad*)

which brings us out
and when the letters
    are reversed

it's revealed
(is born)
as *d'ay*: enough

60
(For indeed the word
Jew — *yehudi* —

is a joining

of *yah* and *d'ay*)

61
And once again
a circle is drawn

(around
that newborn child)

and we've returned

to the issue
of the Lord
    (Shaddai)

62
"I am God Almighty" —
    El Shaddai
    it says

meaning
(according to Rashi)

I'm the one-of-whom
(in whom) there is
enough (*sh'd'ay*)

63
There is, indeed,
enough

and that is
is enough

and there's enough
to this "is"

64
meaning
(in *is*, in *enough*)
    the newborn child

(who has enough

and is himself enough)

65
And this is the firmness
of the breast

(its message)

and we'll
return to this

66
But that
most beautiful man

who leaps

before our eyes
into the water

(the Jordan River)

67
claims that "enough"
(the *d'ay*)
as a fence —

    Shaddai

Meaning: the One
who tells the world —

Enough

68
And this completes
    the definition

of what's enough

as a kind of hedge
to that abundance
(that overflowing
   of Yah)

69
When there's enough

we know
to say Enough
(and vice versa)

and once again
we've drawn a circle —

70
We won't withdraw

from the Name —

we'll recall
that it's enough

71
Recall Shaddai

Recall that is exists
    for *what is*

and offer it
the breast

72
and so it's written

"and you shall look
(upon the birthstools)"

or:
"And the midwives
went in fear (of God)"

73
And the matter's clear—
    that they

indeed witness
all that concealment
(and in this sense
assist in birth)

74
and even literally
listen to
the conversation
    conducted in the womb

And indeed
they're aware of the risk—

75
of that Pharaoh
    in the soul

whose entire being is

substitution,
rejection, abortion

76
And there are infants
who

as embryos

have already
decided

to take their lives

77
You'll hear it when you put
(like Dr. Reynold)

the ultrasound
probe

beneath the belly

78
But
this entire story

   in fact

is taking place
in an open field, a space

79
That
womblike concealment

   is nothing less

than maximal openness

80
the openness of
language,
     creation

and in this sense
   birth

striving for
revelation
   in the flesh

81
This is maximal freedom
that passes

like a scarlet thread

through the hunched
   back of bondage

82
The bondage is
internal

and so at once
made external

and all of life becomes
Ramses and Pithom

83
And in the end
we're speaking of the body

of the semantics
of work

and of
the bride's beauty

84
When she's young
and easily

carries

a pail of water
out to the field

and a pail of fish

85
and then between two pots

"between heaps of stones"
    it says —

"They need them"

86
they lie
with their husbands

    and become with child

"and give birth
beneath the apple tree"

87
And Shifra washes
    (the newborn child)

(rinsing off
the birthwater's blotches)

and Puah clears
out his nostrils

88
Wine is sprinkled
into the nose

as the pure

infant is searched

89
One hundred percent
        an infant

and at the same time

that same (spiritual)
        field
finds expression
as distance

90
The distance creeps in,
the child was born
  just now

    and already

one needs
to hide it away

91
Quick,
let some grandmother

or sister
    (Miriam)

and here
it's Yisrael Epstein—

92
let them take the infant
    and conceal him

and the sequence is:

Encoding
inwardness, otherness

93
Otherwise
he has
    no existence

    and better

even to hand him over
to Pharaoh's daughter

94
And in this sense
(indeed) the Name

can't be seen

and the concealment is
a matter of saving a soul

95
The name (*haShem*)
therefore, takes cover

and becomes something Other:

Mosheh

and this was
the case with Chassyah

96
"I wasn't able"
    (it says)

"to give her

my real name"

97
and not even
"the name I'd taken on"

and that marvelous Yisrael—

98
Yisrael Epstein

"my soul's brother"
            he
calls him
running around in his way

99
to the hospital and back

    and, moved,

presenting himself
as the child's father

100
("Your wife has given birth
    to a baby boy"

he was told

because
of some other Epstein)

101
For it's no longer
possible

to return
to the father—
to the source

(if one doesn't
want to become
    a degenerate)

102
Because the direction
(the meaning)

is forward—

*to be
a father yourself*

103
And to return
　　to the father

　　means

to sink
into illusion and dreams

104
and in the end
to be reduced —

to be a thwarted,
mimicking ape

105
Pharaoh's fatherhood
is better —

that
fatherhood which

is once removed
and can be acquired

106
And it's forbidden
to expose
　　the self

and in this fashion
the lie's function
is —

the lie
defends the self

107
Let's call it a *hijra*
　　that same

　　　　displacement

the infant undergoes
(as a second birth)

108
and he must not
be exposed

　　　　and therefore

he scalds his mouth with a coal

109
and from then on
　　　　will speak

always
through the Other

(and require
Aaron's slippery tongue)

110
He has no
basis

no place

no ground
except The Name!

111
And The Name
is otherness—

    a metonymy

of The Name (*haShem*)
is The Breast (*haShad*)

112
"And therefore
all of Israel's wisdom

let's put it this way,
in short,
    on one leg,

is
the breast's wisdom
    (its study)"

113
And so Pharaoh's daughter too

grew desperate

and they were forced

to rush
the child's mother in

114
It didn't work
with the Egyptian nursemaids

    because

the Lord
"made their teats unfit"

115
And she (Yochaved)
nursed

(him) for two years

it says
"24 months"

116
And this, for her,
    was "enough"

    and so

in nursing
one first of all
    gives "enough"

117
Again,
the milk isn't

    what's essential

but the *enough*

118
and to discover
in the newborn child

that "enough" (which is enough
    —sh'd'ay)

and, as in a mirror,
that enough — within the self

119
And all this
is (interpretation)
    midrash

but nothing

will prosper
without adherence in practice

120
Don't worry
    then

about
fixing the world

but (first of all)
brush the nipples

121
(prior to birth)
with a kind of towel
    and it's important

(so the skin won't crack)

to avoid
using any soap

122
You create
   with your fingers

a kind of "v"

and nurse him
with the nipple

123
For meanwhile
the baby's been born

   and there is no point

in waiting around

124
He's prepared
   to suck

   at once

or the reflex takes some time
(roughly twenty minutes)

125
Nurse —
nurse at once!

and you'll be free
more quickly

of the placenta

126
And put in
   not only the nipple

but the whole

tip of the breast
(the dark round of flesh)

127
Within
3–5 minutes

you'll feel a tickle

and the milk will spurt

128
(At first
it's only a drip

   through

those lactic capillaries)

129
One disposes,
too,

of the black caca
   (the meconium)

if
you nurse at once

130
And that's thanks
   to the colostrum

the feces quickly yellows

becomes a kind
of split pea stew

131
and the odor's reasonable
(at one and the same
   time

   the danger

of jaundice
decreases)

132
And remember
you're granting him

(in every sense —
nutritionally
and in terms
   of digestion)

the ideal food:
mother's milk!

133
You grant
   (as was said)

mother's milk!

On the other hand,
remember:

you're not a restaurant —

134
You're granting

   life
   warmth

continuity
insight and gentleness

137
Food on the whole

135
You've always nursed
(this child)

(as a concept)

and always will

is a kind of midrash

go on nursing
but that nursing

food is
what *disappears*

136
differs
each time
    in conception

138
(disappears in the mouth
in the blood

in the stomach

and will be
internalized
    (in the child

in the intestines
and in the brain)

who'll become
a man
and then a father)

139
So that the essential
    thing about food

and so
it continues

is the level
at which
    it disappears—

the level to which
one lifts it

140
And this, indeed,
the mother knows:

she determines

the levels at which
the milk disappears

141
She guides
the milk

and at once

creates
the meaning (the content)

142
And the axiom is

that milk
always comes

is always ready
always possible

143
And the heart of the matter is

because the milk
is suitable
and quickly digested

the nursing is
(more)
   frequent

144
Nurse often
   (give)

(teach giving
teach acceptance

teach taking)

145
and at any
rate
   at least

every two hours

for if
the breasts swell
   (and harden)

146
there's pain involved

and, on the other hand,
the more frequent the feedings

the more
milk there'll be

147
All the pain
recedes

   there's

less fear of blockage

(in one
of the lactic capillaries)

148
And there's no need
to weigh (the child)

A simple criterion is:

6-8
wet diapers (a day)

149
He needs to gain
   roughly

120
grams a week,

but
forget about that!

150
Let him be
   first of all

like Hannaniah
Mishael and Azariah—

for the milk is holy

151
It doesn't come

to fatten man
alone

to grant him
only sinew and bone

152
The milk —
if you will

is what
     you make (of it)

in the sense of

"I will be
what I will be"

153
Think of what
     the milk is

where to guide
     the milk

and from whence
(it comes)

154
Which is to say
think essence:

essence,
manner, purpose

purpose — which is manner
manner which is essence

155
The milk
is what matters

and what we think
          of it

and here we've spoken
of that same
     breast's wisdom

156
Begin's love
is marvelous

It says

"I stood there . . .
moved and a little embarrassed"

157
"How grateful I was"

he says

"to the good Jews
who had shared in my joy" —

158
several members
of the congregation—

and they were treated

to sliced herring . . .

159
Lord Almighty—

Let me, please,

      wear

Begin's shirt

160
Let me put

Begin's socks

   on my feet

161
so my heart
won't grow haughty

     so I'll not

be numb to feeling
and not be coarse

162
So I'll be
a proper father

a proper husband

so I'll not
curse
   and slur!

163
and so I'll love
Jews—

for
the hardest thing
    is to love
the one who's near

when it's assumed
when it's expected that you will

164
It's easy (in this sense)
   "to love"

your neighbor's children

or
Ishmael's ass—

165
love (to make you mad)
which is unrealizable

which brings about

neither impregnation
nor birth

166
and, anyhow
like a rag

a white
    piece of cloth

flies for a moment in the sky
(above our heads)

167
And after all
everything falls

but first

it's raised
as though in a flash

168
In fact
we didn't see

a thing except
a cluster of letters

and one should hurry
up and read

169
perhaps time

isn't
in that rag—

and it isn't the rag
    that's falling

so much as we are

170
The words don't perish

but we've
in the meantime

moved further away
and the context fades

171
and at one
and the same time

words are derived
   from words

for someone else
to decipher

172
We need, then,

at the appointed time

to do
the right thing

173
The rag lingers
   for a moment

      more

and the word

is *Chassyah*

174
A sacred scribe
   whose craft

is carried out
(not with ink but)

with life itself
and the breath
   of the mouth

175
wrote
the letters
(the signs)
we won't forget:

cheit, samekh, yod, hey —

Cha-ss-ya-h

PART III
(1986–1995)

1

I'm a man
who murdered love

simply
with his own two hands

took
and snapped its neck
        like a lamb

and then, with his fee,
his slaughterer's fee,

promptly turned
into

a *groisser hocham*
—a wise ass—

wise at night
and wise on his ass

—and so

there's Cain and there's Abel
and Joseph and Deborah
and Hamor the Schechemite

and finally

a kind of Aharon Eichmann

wandering around
with — stuck
in his back pocket —

all five scrolls

Lamentations and Ruth
The Song of Songs
    and so on

but waiting
for the firing squad

it's sublime

my eyes

blinded by tears
to take the ringing
    bullets

like the 5
stars of The Bear

I pronounce

life
an act
    of suicide
The New Testament

means
die and die

I can't be
more specific

there's no one
(truly no one)

to whom I'd explain
    the specifics

and whoever there is

to lend an ear
and listen

anyway
turns to nothing:

I'm sobbing
over a neck so white

— it's unbelievable,
unbelievable —

I swear
a neck as white
    as this one

has never existed

I told her:

D., even if they cut off your legs

(I called them "chips")

I'd love you

It was, in fact, a vow ...

You know how far I'd go with her?

Even into apostasy
even into the PLO

I'd —
so I told her —
plain and simple

and all night
(every night)
kiss you

and I'm
    entirely capable
I mean it in all seriousness

of carrying out
just such a total kiss

I'm a man
who, gradually,

has learned

the arts of love

I never
once betrayed my wife

(before the marriage I went
two or three times to whores)

and that's it—
afterwards
year after year

patiently I've learned

patience

I'm able,
how should I put it,

to care for

to care for any
creature requiring care

i.e.,
I take into account
when I stare

at my beloved
the infant
the elder
(the entire design)

and the ill

which follows
from the healthy

and the foul
and the exhausting
and the recurrent

(which is to say:
    The Law)

So instead of saying

"D., look —

here's the mezuzah,

bore
the awl through my ear"

kept to the fence
year after year
I've barked and barked

   at your beauty

I remember a poem
by Alkman —
on Astymeloisa:

"Astymeloisa
won't answer me"
(ouden ameibetai)

"but she holds a garland,

she's like a bright star
cut out of the sky"

and he adds

"like a golden bough,"
etc. (what a wonderful
        poet

you—Astymeloisa!)

My heart's broken
with my saying
(entirely despite myself)

that your nipples
are like thorns

Why
would nipples of thorn

suddenly shatter

a grown man's life?

    And why
didn't you listen

when I said:
    D., come with me —

leave your husband

for me,

a man who, from a mop,

can trick
200 golden proverbs?

Half the night
I can't fall asleep

(from desire)
my balls are sore

but I won't beat off

thinking of Ixion

whom Zeus forgave
and took up

into the sky

where he fell
in love with Hera,

was deceived,

and inseminated
    the goddess —

it was only a cloud
and in the end

he was bound to a wheel
for all eternity

like me
bound to the wheel
    of thinking

bound to your name

5

From an infant I've turned
into a fat man

my hair's going gray
and becoming a kind of
    useless rag

when I eat
I run my tongue

along my dentures

on the other hand
I'm awfully young, and funny,
cordial, my hands are good

erotic — in the ancient sense,
        the daemonic —

and my back is strong
despite one lousy disc

I strained
when I picked up a stone idiotically

My brother's tanned legs
(he boasted of, philandered with)
are long since eaten, whereas mine

mine are o.k. — last night I even dreamed
I was called in to play fullback

Unfortunately, my scrotum's shot

(once it would shrink up in the cold
like a crop)

and my penis I admire
fascinated by its white liquid

I've learned in my life to use it wisely

and your belly is like a leveled bowl
and at its tip are leaves of laurel

6

Within myself I've discovered
an opening

imagine for a moment the cave
of Pan at Banias

and was astonished
at the shiftings of meaning there

that what's wanting we call an opening

and the opening we call the past

that the past has the supple body
of a young woman

and she told me
what no one ever told me
(what I've always wanted to be told)

and as much as she told me
so the girl in me grew

deepening, and deepening, and deepening
the past

and, accordingly, the openness

and, as it were,
all became wanting

11

You've impoverished me and forced me
to impoverish you in return

and from here on in the world
will evolve as an abscess

of sexual greed — I'll
definitely manage to seduce you

I'll flatter you
I'll coax you into exposing a nipple

I'll speak to your heart
asking

to let me kiss your rear

already now I'm
changing my ideals

choosing new gods

for I'm not going out
except so as not
            to return —

which is to say

the mode, the ethos
the place—the placing,
   word, and genius—
    are changing)

Listen D.:

the gods get annoyed

they're fragments
of ourselves

and we're cosmic fragments
and other fragments
and still others

and regret's pointless
and wealth and poverty are pointless—everything's
     wealth and everything's poverty—

like an old cloth of gold
  we'll tear gods

when I put my lips to your asshole

20

I'm a love poet

who said to his beloved
honey, you stay in bed

and I'll
go get some eggs

except that my going
has lasted twenty years

twenty years
I've been out getting eggs

though I did believe
the act most appropriate
    for a love poet

to say to his beloved
honey, you stay in bed

and I'll
go get some eggs

21

This love, this addiction—to eggs

has cost me this—
I can't stand them any longer

I want diamonds, diamonds

diamonds big as ostrich eggs

though as I say it
I'm talking again about eggs

Ach—because I know only about eggs
know, in fact, only how to hate

26

My two hands compose poems,
miles of poems,

from within your body —

remember, D., the honey

in the lion's
carcass, the honey . . .

the miles
jab at the sky

stab at the clouds

tickle the stars

man's such a schmuck —

a poem stuck up God's ass —

thwarted, feasting, thwarted, feasting

vi

So long as I don't fuck you

I'm filled to the brim
and remain full

and stand before your life
like a Seraph

"the appearance of brightness,
as the color of electrum"

electrifying actually

threatening actually
to bring about marvelous changes within you

to bestow upon you
vitality rhythms and meanings

though all this ground —
a kind of plot of Mother Earth —

is rendered
not of this time and not of this place

and an artificial desert's formed
wherein you stand, like Pasiphae,

a charming and beautiful girl
who lost her mind and fell in love
    with the bull of Minos

(she was that same king's wife)

Daedalus the crafty, the artist

placed her nude
within a model cow

he constructed of planks
and probably planed and smoothed

so that the marvelous pure-white bull
which burst forth from the sea as a gift from Poseidon

that god-like bull
with which at the moment I identify

wouldn't wound its testicles

when it bent its huge body
and thrust its maleness
into that work of art made of wood

that artificial cunt
across which exists

the warm natural cunt of the woman

and these are the two sisters
(art, let's say, and life)

and without crossing through one
there's no reaching the other

ix

A cow gives milk

the hen's gift—
        an egg

An idiot
asks of the cow an egg

or
with greedy hands

looks for a teat
on the hen;

you fool,
go skip in the thistles

and get out of my hair.

All of the above
concerning myself:

I picture you

born of the sea-foam,
curves upon curves,

and ahh, what legs!

If I
had several members

my desire would never
say enough ...

What a fool,

I thought we'd meet

holding maps
of two different planets
        in our hands

You said:

I love you

I took my bag
and went out to meet you

but you were talking
Indian-talk

and in Indian-talk
love's

a playful tickle
around the navel

and nothing more,

a tickle

and after
you turn on your bum

and light a fire

or fuss with the kettle

indeed —

a playful thing

I didn't understand

"I love you"

was only a story

the story — not about me

but about yourself

and a story is always
a story spun out of (within) a story

someone else is speaking

I'm thinking of Philomela

whose brother-in-law raped her
and tore out her tongue

and she wove a pattern
into a piece of cloth

her story in glorious colors

and became in the end a nightingale

which is to say, like you,
she told a story with a bob of her tail

— that tail I don't mean to belittle

(in fact it's all I can manage,
        and desire, to catch hold of

like the rest of the world) ...

A man full of desire and full of words

I'm gazing
with blinking eyes at my cloth

I've told a story about myself,

and in the end
what's left of me? A tail

THE CAR

I've put all my belongings into the back of the car
right now, in fact, I live in the car
I have money for gas
and a wide glass windshield
I take care of the tires and inflate them
then set out in search of a mate

"THE LAST YEAR OF MY MARRIAGE"

The last year of my marriage reminds me of a porch
in the small town of Rishpon I passed by chance as a child
It was almost evening, a middle-aged farmer and farmer's wife
were sitting on chairs (the man was wearing a gray casquette)
and two huge sacks of peanuts rested between their knees

THE PRAYER BOOK

For years I've wanted to write a prayer book
Why? Because I've learned
that the solid hangs upon nothingness
Because I've found that the sentence is a kind of petition
And because I've found that in all that I've said
in all that I've said I've said only thank you
So, little by little,
in fact I've written that book
and today it weighs some two hundred pounds
and soon it will celebrate its fiftieth birthday
and yesterday I bought it shoes

A CROWN

Masha, my mother, swallowed a crown
She shut herself up in the bathroom once or twice
and with some pointy tool poked around
in a bowl full of stools
From those good old days behind the door
I hear that click click click ...
It's fantastic — that each object and purpose contains
a difference that becomes an addition
The fruit of that clicking is diligence, and that's the crown

THE DOOR

My neighbor's musical instrument of choice is the door—
at first I thought it a major nuisance
and then I saw it was really part
of a kind of sonata for percussion
and the aggravation dissolved: now I observe
how skillful this soloist is in her entrance and exit

"I'M OBLIGED TO HONOR"

I'm obliged to honor your cunt with my tongue
Like the prophet who swallows the scroll
and Gideon's soldiers who kneel and lick,
the poet speaks only of things that he tastes
Each taste in his mouth comes to innocence
He builds a fence against all that's coarse
and coarseness fades from the coarse;
as Pindar put it, his task is to guard like a dragon
the Muses' apples, and the apples given at the gods' wedding
He has only to bow his head in humility
between his beloved's thighs
as his mouth bestows on her cunt a dewfall of kisses

"ZIVA"

Ziva,
when will I touch the pair of sparrows nesting there in your lap?
I'm arguing now with the purists, those drinkers of chilled white wine
I prefer the beverage that issues straight from your mouth
or at the end of the month, when the gluttonous penis
descends to your pussy, gets dirty with jelly and drunk with must
Not even Magellan traveled as far as the heart and mind
moving between the holes of the cunt and bum —
and with me that route is daily bread
Like the Centaur who took Deianeira over the river
my fate follows the path I take with my tongue
Basho climbed Mt. Kashima
and left for posterity the full moon,
while I'll bequeath to the world
a diamond of spit I've set in your omphalos, Ziva

"I POUND MY EGGHEAD"

I pound my egghead hoping it will tell me
why I love your buttocks so
For years I sat in the National Library
reading the chapters of Plato's *Republic*
and all that I read led me on
from one good thought to another and better
    For each I found the proper material
I fathered children and cleaned their caca,
bought a house and planted a vine,
wrote a book and raised up students
In short, I could have just turned my head
and found the signpost beneath my back,
instead of marching for twenty-five years
in order to get to the rear

15
My heart's so full of shit,
and that's the quality in me that sings:

Yesterday we fought with shouts
about money and you got hit—

and your glasses flew off—
but the day before

I came to you with my tongue
from the ankle up to your ears

an hour and a half or more
(my cock, like the locomotive

in *La bête humaine* by Renoir
pulling the mouth and face around and around

—inside, forward and back—
the body rushing it blood

like fire within me and coal);
you screamed, and bit my lip,

like in Herodotus, where the story's told
of the female flying snake

which, as it comes to a climax,
pierces the throat of its mate

24

Day after day after day I look on while you're lying down
beside me like a low hill, naked, tufts of grass having grown

here and there along its slopes. And beyond that, I'm certain,
something's happening: armies are being deployed, Medean and Persian;

Xerxes sits on his throne, with a silver cup in his hand,
or a young man is killing his uncles – the boy from Calydon –

in order to give Atalanta the hide of the wild boar;
and maybe there's also a jungle looming, or a desert floor

where the Phoenix emerges or begins to fade in the sand.
Above that most ideal of landscapes I'll never ascend,

I'll never seek out what's clearly beyond
the body on which I've kissed each limb –

and day after day after day, so long as my eyes stay open,
they'll graze on that hill, on that back, on that bottom

28

When you were twenty, not wanting to miss even an hour
with your lover who was set to leave for Algiers

you faked a serious stomach ache and played the part so well
that you were taken from the studio to the hospital

Hôtel Dieu's emergency room, where, despite your denials,
an overly zealous doctor removed your appendix after he'd put you
    under.

Now you're asleep, and beside you I'm wide awake, still
thinking about that scar, that pale seal

branded across your belly for love of a distant and different man
who long ago drowned in the sea. Lord, how I envy him

who, packing a bag and adding some books and trousers,
suddenly gets a call and goes to answer.

Again and again I'm tempted to follow the way
he takes along that river, toward L'Île de la Cité:

with me he buys you flowers, climbs the stairs to the right ward
and the room that's draped in white, looks around, then moves toward

your bed, and there inside me you're waiting for him, breathless —
and he smothers your smiling mouth, like a pomegranate, in kisses . . .

CONSECRATION

The floor's three by three. As in a cathedral
with only a single seat, his gaze climbs
along the length of a pipe and toward the sublime
up to a cast-iron organ attached on high to the wall.

The boy, lowering his eyes to where his pants
lie crumpled on the floor in a kind of detachment,
waits for the bowels' thunder, the stench of excrement,
and the spray of water that always splatters his ass.

He sends a hand back around to the hole,
the issue of which he'll never share with a soul
and, like Jonathan dipping his stick into the hive's

comb, he draws to his lips a fleck of the manna,
licks his finger clean, removing the sign,
and rises, utterly pure and alone, like no one alive.

"I'VE ALWAYS MISSED OUT"

I've always missed out on the prettiest girls;
only after they've screwed in every hole and position
do they come to me for help with their poems, or a lesson,
and I tell them of Phoinix, whose lips dripped pearls

of wisdom and how, in exchange for the knowledge, he'd usually
get a comfortable bed with sheets of lambskin and, if he were lucky,
hear—in an adjacent tent—Patróklos
making love with Iphis, and Diomêdê with Akhilleus.

So I won't get to sleep with the prettiest girls.
I'll fix their lines, put up with their stupid chatter,
and, late at night, comfort myself as I stick my finger

into my rear then pull it out and know, lifting it up to my nose,
that the biggest, blackest, and totally most mysterious
dick in the world is lying here in this bed writing my poems.

"IF ALL THE WORLD WERE CONTAINED"

If all the world were contained in an automat
I'd never choose juice or even hot chocolate,
but what my balls are always craving instead.
Nearly thirty-one years have passed in my head

and my spirit's still depressed about having
hesitated when Anna Traphelt crouched over
my face and ordered me to lick her. I may be a madman,
but ever since then my tongue has grown longer

the further that reddish triangle of springy hair
recedes into the distance, as though in Plato's parable
of the cave, from that room at the Hotel Notre Dame,

and, on the horizon, it sheds and takes on form:
just yesterday it seemed like a honeycomb,
and today it's only a star, its sweetness gone.

HAPPINESS

The rain comes down and rattles the roof's red tiles
and the heart, too, longs to be decently wet.
I'm reading Aristotle again — who says that the good
is that to which all mankind aspires,

and the supreme good, in its way, is like a pastry
one bakes with all earthly matter and savvy
until it rises to a condition that we call happiness,
and a man sits as though sufficient unto himself —

the ring of beloved souls around him as air,
knowing the golden mean between extremes,
and, like me, listening to the sound of the rain,

reading and thinking, at ease in his armchair —
when his finger finds in his pants pocket a hole,
burrows down to his member, and starts to twirl.

PART IV

(2007—2008)

TANYA'S WALKING AROUND

Tanya's walking around the apartment

Tanya's taking
a bottle of soda out of the fridge

Tanya's sitting down on the sofa
with a bag of sunflower seeds
to read the paper

Tanya's looking out the window
at the trees

Tanya's checking to see if the pigeon
is still sitting on her eggs in the pot

Tanya's coming out of the shower
wrapped in a dark-blue towel

Tanya's having something to eat
before she goes to sleep —

tuna salad on a slice of bread

CLOCKS

According to the black clock
left in the room
with Tanya's belongings
it's now 8:55 in the evening

and she has time enough still
to write another recommendation
or answer her mail

My watch shows
3:55 in the morning
I'll read another page
on Schopenhauer as Educator

then lie down and go to sleep

MY HEART'S AS EMPTY AS THIS PAIL

My heart's as empty as this pail
without you

I'll lean
over the bathtub
and fill it with water

and soak
the washrag in it

then mop the floor

HAPPINESS

I.

I'm happy with
my love for my wife

and even though her body
now lies in the ground

they can't take
away the joy

II.

Everything passes,
Gershuni tells me

filling my heart
with joy

TANYA'S CRYING

Tanya learned not to tilt
her head in embarrassment

She's standing tall in a cheap leather coat
but her voice is choked with tears

when she answers the question about
Gaza becoming a prison

— *What's happening to me?*
Could they feel I was crying?

— *They could feel it*

— *It's been happening to me lately*
It also happened in Adelaide

MARCH 30, 2007

Death, my friend,
Uncle Death,
good morning

Pour a little milk for me
into the cornflakes

Death, my friend,
Uncle Death,
good evening

Go to the drugstore
down the street

and bring me condoms

MOURNING

The death of that finest,
most beautiful woman

I'll forget
in five minutes

because my eyes
are over my chest

The white satin panties
the pants I'd taken to be shortened
by the Ukrainian seamstress
and the rest of her clothes

I've stuffed
into six shiny trash bags
to have them handed out to the poor

I won't survive
on crumbs from a chocolate cake
in a plastic wrapper

Greetings,
O fresh loaves of bread
and brand-new breasts

CLASSIFIED

I'm a widower
who's looking
for a new woman

She should be good
and pretty

I can make her
stuffed Cornish game hens

and we'll eat while watching a movie

At night we'll talk in the dark

I have a soft, sand-colored bathrobe

I'm happy

My dick always gets stiff

SEPARATION

You kissed me,
then crossed Seventh Ave
wearing my hat with the visor

and without looking back
you walked an entire block

along the opposite side of the street
until you went into Loehmann's

while I still stood there at the corner
of Seventeenth—

unable to take my eyes off you

I JUST WANTED TO LOOK AT TANYA

I just wanted to look at Tanya—
how she stood tall in her coat
at the end of the hall
on her department's floor
as I came out of the elevator;
how she lit her cigarette
at the entrance archway
as we walked out to Broadway;
how her legs appeared
beneath the dressing-room door
as she tried on pants
at Urban Outfitters;
how she looked at the menu
at the Russian restaurant;
how she'd bring me coffee
in a plastic cup
along the red carpet
at the Quad Cinema
while I waited
in the chair by the rope.
I just wanted to look at her
that Thursday,
and that final night
at the morgue
in Suffolk, New York,
725 Veterans Memorial Highway,
as I pulled back the sheet.

WIDOWER

I'm a widower
and will stay a widower,
because I'm a widower
and my wife has gone away

and my wife is gone,
gone

her table too
isn't her table
and her husband, as well,
is not her husband

TANYA ALWAYS COMES

Tanya always comes

Her key pecks at the lock
and *my* keys fall
with a clatter to the carpet

O those eyes that shine
in the hallway's darkness
O the kisses

She puts her bag
by the kitchen counter

O bottle of beer
that she takes out of the fridge

settling into the armchair
and taking off her shoes

TANYA'S NO MORE

Tanya's no more
Tanya's no more

and so I wander
and so I wander

with a sack full of cash
with a sack full of cash

with a huge hole in my heart
with a huge hole in my heart

with 15 pipes
with 15 pipes

from woman to woman
from woman to woman

from apartment to apartment
from apartment to apartment

with black Prada shoes
with black Prada shoes

with brown Prada shoes
with brown Prada shoes

tonight I'll read *Zadig*
tonight I'll read *Zadig*

THE TRUTH

The truth was tall and thin
and behind the glass partition
took a shower before my eyes

and naked came to bed
so I would enter into her
and she into me

so she'd embrace me
and I her

She'd stride like a horse through the living room

toward the table
to eat the lettuce
salad I'd made her

IT'S GOOD WITHOUT TANYA

The salmon sandwich
spread with cheese

says to me:
"It's good without Tanya"

and I don't throw it away
as I cross the bridge

then eat while walking
along the canal

TANYA WAS GORGEOUS

"Tanya was gorgeous"
I tell Moishe

and he raises his head
over the bowl of bean soup

and just as he did ten years ago
he looks at me and says:

"Not everyone thinks so."

YOU'D LIKE TO KNOW

You'd like to know
how it feels to live without you

Like a man falling
from the hundredth floor

who sees, in a window,
a beautiful woman undressing

SCHIPHOL

I.
I peer to the side in the taxi
to Schiphol Airport

Always at moments like these
we'd sit back and grin:

Now we'll have time
to be together

II.
We loved each other so much,
so much

Now it's good to sit and smoke
beside the two bags

with the yellow bulldozer
in the lot below

THE MAN WHO LISTENS

On the white couch
we smoked grass in the dark.
Slowly I started to speak.
You need to learn, she said,
to become a man who listens.
And I saw him there in the shadows
in the corner by the stereo
wearing a reed skirt
and peering like a bushman
from the amplifier bulb.
And what does a man who listens want,
she asked, and I didn't know.
What does a man who listens want?
What does a man who listens want?
I looked toward the red, glistening eye
of the one who listens.
He wants to listen, I said.
No, she answered, no —
stressing every word —
the man who listens
wants a conversation.
And why is that? she asked.
And I waited for her to tell me.
Because the man who listens wants
to be a man in conversation. And again:
the man who listens wants
to be a man in conversation.

At once I agreed.
And what sort of conversation? she asked.
I didn't answer.
An Eastern dialogue?
A Western dialogue?
Socratic? she asked.
I wavered. An Eastern dialogue ...
No, she said, a Socratic dialogue.
Yes, I said,
that's what I've really wanted,
a Socratic dialogue,
but I wasn't sure.
And two years later,
on that last night, in March, in Montauk,
during our final joint together,
as we argued (over whether
or not to turn the music off
along with the flickering screen
and look in silence at the ocean)
she said to me sadly
I see you've completely forgotten
what you'd learned
about the man who listens —
and I no longer have the strength
to teach you again from the start.
Why? I said, I'm prepared to learn.
And she spoke and spoke

and repeated what she'd said
over and over,
and I grew quiet, and she calmed down,
and I became a man who listens
and would listen to her no more.

AFTERWORD

ON BEING A POET: SOME NOTES FOR A TALK

1. There's a difference between writing a good poem and being a poet. It's possible to learn how to write a good poem. There are models, and one can work out variations on them within a certain range. But to be a poet involves something else and altogether different. Keats called it negative capability. I call it a capacity for sustenance – to sustain and be sustained, which is to say, to continue. And to continue means to always make and say something different.

2. And that isn't necessarily pleasant. On the one hand I love poetry, and over the course of many years it has become a regular part of me. So it's clear that I'm expected to play a certain role, and I understand when they tell me: "Behave yourself, show a little respect!" But the fact is that I'm not "respectable" – I'm notorious. The audience is thirsty for respectability, for legitimacy, for cultural authority, all the more so here in Israel, in a place where the absence of legitimacy and respect are so glaring. But now, facing an audience grown accustomed to being obedient, one wants to say, of all things, something annoying and critical, to get under the skin of what's respectable and, yes, enjoy the vulgarity of it and be a little wild. Scandalous behavior has characterized the lyric since the days of the Dionysian *komos* (the archaic revel) and the iambic poems of Archilochus and Hipponax. *Iambizein* means, in Greek, to mock, to scorn. The ethical function of poetry is to praise and approve, and so – to reject and condemn. This is particularly conspicuous in the first two books of the *Iliad* – that it's impossible to praise without rejection and condemnation. In *King Lear*, there's a scene that's full of abuse, and also in *Troilus and Cressida*.

3. Poetry appeals as a product to which importance accrues. As a kind of boredom bearing prestige. It easily finds itself flattering an audience thirsty for the respectable. The demand for it is fixed, especially when literature is written and marketed as part of a state-sponsored project of moral disregard and denial. It serves as a kind of greenhouse, under which it's possible to adorn oneself with a feeling of spiritual cleanliness. The absurd slaughter of World War I, the patriotism of the herd, the obtuseness, the obsequiousness of the intellectual class, formed the background to the scandals staged during the time of Tristan Tzara and the Dadaists, to Mayakovsky's provocations, to the antipoems of Nicanor Parra.

4. As I see it, the situation in Israel is similar today, after several glorious years of "the war on terror." But in the past as well, in better times, I preferred the critical sense, humor, hyperbole, an idiotic simplemindedness, everything that was alien to "poetry" and removed the quotation marks around it. A poet first of all has to know how to stop being a poet, to go out into the street, to look at the cars, to understand that a poem in reality isn't important, that it's hypocritical to overvalue verse. Because poetry is first of all that going out, that freedom, a radical gesture, as Raymond Queneau observed: "Ça a toujours kékchose d'extrême / un poème" ("It's always something extreme / a poem"). And this touches upon the difference between writing a good poem and being a poet.

5. A poet thinks and changes, and the poem is a gesture in the direction of that change. The poem resides in that movement. It never ends; one always has to reread it, over and over, because that gesture is an answer to the ongoing need for ethical reorientation (to distinguish, to decide, to move, to oppose).

6. Therefore the dynamic components of a poem are deceptive. Critics, professors, and teachers of workshops often have trouble identifying them. It would seem, at first, that it's sufficient to choose one's words with care. This is an element that draws attention to itself. People fall in love with the words of the poem and its images, as though they were walking across a solid floor of words. But more important still are the words one *doesn't* choose. This is how gaps are formed in a poem. In the gaps between the words the poem takes on its character, is set into motion, interrupted, saved from infatuation with its own reflection; it encounters something else, receives feedback, finds otherness, absorbs critique. It navigates along these gaps and spaces, passes from one thing to another, from one register to another. By means of these gaps the pitch is created along which what's said ascends or slides (that's its topography, its dynamism). This also touches on rhythm, which is life, the physical-gymnastic distinction of the poem that moves and assumes weight and authenticity by means of timing (vis-à-vis each word) and within time.

7. Another important factor is appropriate dimension, or size and sense of proportion. A poem has a given size or dimension, and only within that size is it true. It's the same as with drawing and architecture. The modest airport in Cairo is built to the right proportions, likewise Schiphol Airport near Amsterdam. It's huge, granted, but entirely functional and teeming with life. The new Ben Gurion Airport near Tel Aviv (which bears the name of Israel's first prime minister) has no sense of size or proportion, and in this respect the poem I wrote about it (p. 32) speaks not only about the state that built it as a monument, but also about the use of hyperbole in poetry. The core of the poem is a spinelike proportional structure that appears as a vertical column of words at the start of each line: "Lord, / what a / corridor / of marble, / stone / and glass, / so high / and empty, / on the way / toward / the suitcases." The multiple repetitions that follow in each line express the arrogance and presumption of the monument, the nouveau-riche cult of marble, glass, enormity, etc. On the other hand, on the level of poetry there's an inverse emphasis. The essential core was composed as a kind of ars poetica, along the lines of William Carlos Williams's well-known "so much depends / upon // a red wheel / barrow // glazed with rain / water // beside the white / chickens." These poetics (which have become conservative) are opened up in the poem about the new airport through a kind of Dadaistic or Gertrude Stein-like hyperbole. The poem isn't just an illustration (of the inflated and aggressive structure) but also an act that liberates the words from the burden of the ideological structure that has been imposed on them.

8. Syntax (composition) is, as I see it, the most important element within the array of linguistic materials. What leads people astray and deceives, in a political sense, isn't exactly the (fraudulent and laundered) words that are chosen, but above all the *syntaxis,* the composition, the conception that links the facts. I'm sensitive first of all to composition. When the syntax is working, when there's composition and conception, there's a poem. But composition of course is linked in the wider sense to an understanding of the real. In order to compose, to put together, a poet has to possess a good understanding of the links between things, between facts – emotional and ethical facts, the facts around him and in the world. Therefore he has to have the ability to judge, to form an opinion, to think, to argue and articulate a position. If you're obedient, you won't understand a thing; you'll understand only what you're supposed to understand, like a student in a classroom with windows along just a single wall. In order to understand and argue (to compose things, to draw conclusions), one has to have the ability to dismantle definitions – the walls and categories that have been constructed, and are being constructed, all around us as obstacles (or roadblocks) and containers of identity.

9. It's possible to sum up what I've tried to say with this point: As I see it, the most important characteristic in poetry is the utterance, the argument. When I read a poem I look first of all for what is being claimed, for the *logos.* What is asked of us is that we become obedient, that we take up what is acceptable, that we stop thinking, which is to say, that we not argue. This, after all, is the subject of Socrates' apology. He too would certainly agree that the poet is he or she who possesses the *logos.*

February 2007

NOTES

Part I

"Rypin"

Pronounced *Ri-PEEN*. A town in north-central Poland. Umberto Saba is the Italian poet of partial Jewish ancestry; with the occupation of Italy by German forces in 1943, he went into hiding with his family in Florence, where they frequently changed dwellings.

"Hope"

Karmei Avdat: A vineyard and vacation spot in the Negev desert.

Amira and Neta: Amira Hass, the journalist, and Neta Golan, an activist. Both have worked for many years in the interest of peace, often at considerable risk.

Rachel: Rachel Corrie (1979–2003), an American member of the International Solidarity Movement who traveled to the Gaza Strip during the Second Intifada. While protesting against the destruction of Palestinian homes by the Israeli army in Gaza, she was killed by an armored bulldozer operated by the Israel Defense Forces.

Mas'ha checkpoint: In the West Bank, south of Qalqilya. A peace camp was set up there in 2003.

"Hebrew Culture"

Pinkie: Pinhas (Pinkie) Zuaretz was the head of the Gaza Southern Command during the Second Intifada and implemented harsh and collective retaliatory measures for Palestinian violence, including razing homes along the border and, according to the *Guardian* (June 28, 2005, Chris McGreal), rewriting the rules of engagement "to permit soldiers to shoot children as young as 14." He had part of his leg blown off by a roadside bomb while patrolling in Gaza in 2005.

Bogie: The nickname of General Moshe Ya'alon, who was chief of staff of the IDF from 2002–05 and led the efforts to quell the Second Intifada. He became known for his extreme pronouncements, such as: "The Palestinian threat harbors cancer-like attributes that have to be severed. There are all kinds of solutions to cancer. Some say it's necessary to amputate organs but at the moment I am applying chemotherapy" (*Ha'aretz*, August 27, 2002).

At the time of this book's publication, he was deputy prime minister and minister of strategic affairs in the Netanyahu cabinet.

"Four Roadblocks"
Marda, Zeita, Yasuf, and Iskaka are Palestinian villages on the West Bank that are regularly cut off from the main roads leading through the territories and to Jewish settlements such as Ariel and Kfar Tapu'ah.

"Sharon Resembles a Person"
This poem was written several years before Ariel Sharon suffered the January 4, 2006 stroke that left him unconscious and on life support.

"What's Spinoza?"
Mr. Mofaz: A former chief of staff, Ret. General Sha'ul Mofaz was minister of defense from 2002 through 2006.

"The Reason to Live Here"
Samaria: Capital of the northern kingdom of Israel in the ninth and eighth centuries b.c.e., following the split of the Israelite kingdom after the death of Solomon. In the biblicizing terminology of the Greater Israel movement and the Israeli government, it is now the Hebrew name for the northern part of the West Bank.
Melampus: In Greek mythology, the first mortal endowed with prophetic powers. The story of the serpents is told in Apollodorus I:9.11.

"Elections: Israel, 2001"
The two candidates in this election were Ehud Barak and Ariel Sharon. There was a widespread movement among the Israeli Left to cast blank ballots in protest at the lack of a better alternative. This poem appeared in *Ha'aretz* just prior to election day.

"Our Land"

fallah: Arabic for peasant or farmer; plural *fellahin.*

jallabiya: Arabic for the cotton gown or robe worn by men.

legend told by Bialik: A story from the poet Haim Nahman Bialik's *Book of Legends* that illustrates the Solomonic verse from Proverbs 18:21: "Death and life are in the power of the tongue." In the story, the King of Persia is ordered by his doctor to obtain the milk of a lioness in order to cure a malady that is devouring him. When his own men say that the task is beyond them, he turns to Solomon, the wisest of kings. One of Solomon's men cleverly works out a plan and obtains the milk from the lioness. That night, in a dream, the leader of the group hears the parts of his body arguing over which is supreme and which made the greatest contribution to the solution of the problem – the legs, the hands, the eyes, the heart, the tongue, and so on. When he presents the milk to the King, he finds himself saying, despite himself: "My Lord, we have just now returned and brought, as you requested, the milk of the bitch-dog." The King recoils in anger and sentences him to hang. On the way to the gallows, as all the parts of the body are trembling in fear, the tongue says to them: "And now do you see who reigns supreme?" In the end, the tongue also talks the King out of hanging the man.

"As We Were Marching"

Rafi'ah: A neighborhood in Gaza.

Shenkin: Shenkin, Labor, Bograshov, and King George are all streets in Tel Aviv.

Death to the Arabs: A slogan often chanted at Israeli soccer games and after terrorist bombings, and commonly encountered as graffiti.

"2004"

Tali Fahima (b. 1976) is an Israeli woman of North African descent who grew up in a poor working-class town in the south of Israel. In 2004 she was arrested and charged with supplying classified information to the Jenin commander of the Palestinian al-Aqsa Martyrs' Brigade. At first confined to administrative detention, she was eventually tried and convicted. She spent several years in jail.

"Failure"

This ... war: The second Lebanon War, which began on July 12, 2006. It was widely supported by the Israeli public and the vast majority of its prominent intellectuals and writers.

Olmert: Ehud, prime minister at the time. Haim Ramon was minister of defense.

Chimichanga: A casual but upscale Mexican restaurant in Tel Aviv.

"Gaza: Two Poems"

After eighteen months of closure, Operation Cast Lead began in December 2008.

PART II

"Education"

The Altalena: A cargo ship carrying weapons and munitions which the Irgun (the right-wing paramilitary Jewish resistance group founded during the British Mandate) was trying to smuggle into the country. The ship was sunk by the newly created Israeli army in a gesture intended to subdue renegade paramilitary factions. Sixteen Irgun fighters were killed. Menahem Begin boarded the ship in an act of solidarity with his fellow Irgun members and refused to leave it until all the wounded had been evacuated.

Dov Sadan: One of Israel's most famous literary critics at the time.

"Begin"

This excerpt is from a 1986 book-length poem about Menahem Begin, the veteran leader of the Jewish underground in Palestine and of the conservative Herut Party in Israel. Long ridiculed while in the political opposition, Begin was—in a major political revolution—elected prime minister in 1979, becoming the first leader of a right-wing government in Israeli history. In one of his greatest acts of literary provocation, Shabtai, who had long been identified with the political Left in Israel, came out with a two-part paean to the man the left most reviled. Shabtai has said that he was drawn not so much to the fact that Begin had made peace with Egypt (something that goes unmentioned in the poem), but to Begin's warmth and sense of paternal responsibility—qualities Shabtai felt lacking on the Left.

The poem employs a traditional Hebraic method of interpretation – midrash – and takes as its "sacred text" two pages from Begin's autobiography, *The Revolt*. The first page (part I of the poem, not translated here), treats the episode of Begin's Jewish underground unit breaking into the British munitions depot in Palestine and stealing weapons and ammunition. This the poet likens to, among other things, the high priest entering the holy of holies on the Day of Atonement. Part II treats Begin's account of the birth of his daughter while he was in hiding from the British, who had placed Begin at the top of their Most Wanted list. The prose passage on page 58 is from Begin's autobiography and serves as Scripture for his commentary.

4: Verfluchte Jude is "damn Jew" or "accursed Jew" – a common anti-Semitic slur.

11: Cf. Hosea 2:15: "I will give her vineyards from thence, and the valley of Achor for a door of hope; and she shall respond there, as in the days of her youth, and as in the day when she came up out of the land of Egypt."

18: Hayot (givers of life) is from the Midrash, *Genesis Rabbah* 82.

19–26: The stories that follow are from the Talmud – *Berakhot* 62a. Rabbi Akiva was one of the great sages of Talmudic times. Ben Azzai and Rav Cahana are other sages who figure prominently in the Talmud and the Midrash.

29: Rav was one of the leading Babylonian scholars and the founder of the important academy of Sura. He was also known as Rav Aba.

31: Brisk is the Yiddish name for the Belorussian town of Brest, where Begin was born in 1913. His parents perished there in the Holocaust, and his brother disappeared without a trace.

39: The German philosopher is Heidegger, who claimed that we forget being itself and remember only beings. Shabtai reverses that formulation in this passage.

44: 1 Kings 3:16. This is the story of Solomon and the two women fighting over the single living child.

54: The Mekhilta is an important collection of midrashim (plural of midrash) that comments on the Book of Exodus.

55: The name "Hoshea" (i.e., Hosea) became "Yehoshua" (or Joshua) when "yah" (an abbreviation of God's name) was added to it, indicating the presence of God in the man's life, just as the addition of the letter "hey" to Avram and Sarai created Avraham and Sarah. The Midrash states that after the performance of good deeds, a letter was added to the names of these biblical heroes. Mekhilta, *Tractate Amalek*, chapter 3.

66: The story of that "beautiful man" appears in the Talmud, *Baba Metzia* 84a, and involves R. Johanan and Reish Lakish.

87: Shifra and Puah are the first recorded "Hebrew midwives" (Exodus, 1:15).

PART III

"Love: 6"
Banias is a cave in northern Galilee associated with the cult of Pan.

"The Last Year of My Marriage"
Rishpon is a small farming community (est. 1936) on the coastal plain of Israel.

"Metazivika: 15"
The story of the female flying snake appears in Herodotus, *The Persian Wars*, Book III.

"Metazivika: 24"
The story of Xerxes watching the battle at Salamis is from *The Persian Wars*, Book VIII. The episode of the boy of Calydon and the boar is told in *The Iliad*, Book IX.

"I've Always Missed Out"
Phoinix, Patróklos, Akhilleus, and Diomêdê appear together in Book IX of *The Iliad*.

PART IV

The poems of Part IV were written in the wake of the sudden death of Tanya Reinhart, the poet's second wife. Reinhart died of heart failure on March 17, 2007, in Montauk, New York. She was 64. A student of Noam Chomsky, Reinhart became a renowned linguist and cultural commentator in her own right.

She was an outspoken critic of Israeli government policies in the occupied territories and was, as Chomsky noted after her death, "on the front line of direct resistance to intolerable actions, an organizer and a participant." She would be remembered, he said, "not only as a resolute and honorable defender of the rights of Palestinians, but also as one of those who have struggled to defend the moral integrity of her own Israeli society, and its hope for decent survival."

"Tanya's Crying"
Adelaide, Australia, where Reinhart delivered the Edward Said Memorial Lecture in 2006.

"Classified"
Like many of Shabtai's poems, this one was published on the literary pages of *Ha'aretz*, the country's leading newspaper.

"I Just Wanted to Look at Tanya"
Reinhart taught for many years at Tel Aviv University and the University of Utrecht. When she died, she was just beginning the term of a new appointment as Global Distinguished Professor at NYU.

"Tanya's No More"
Zadig: A short novel by Voltaire that presents life as endless trial. Its hero is a young, decent, well-off, and well-educated Babylonian who learns just how hard it is to be happy in a world where things inevitably go wrong in spite of one's efforts to do right.

BIOGRAPHICAL NOTES

One of the leading poets in Israel today, AHARON SHABTAI was born in 1939 in Tel Aviv and grew up there and on Kibbutz Merhavia. After his military service, he studied Greek and philosophy at the Hebrew University in Jerusalem, the Sorbonne, and at Cambridge, and went on to teach theater studies and literature at the Hebrew University in Jerusalem and Tel Aviv University. He is the foremost translator of Greek drama into Hebrew, having published over thirty plays in annotated editions, and he has received the Prime Minister's Prize, the Tchernikhovsky Prize, and the Leah Goldberg Award for his work as both a poet and a translator. Shabtai is the author of eighteen volumes of poetry in Hebrew. Two previous selections of his work have appeared in English translations by Peter Cole: *Love & Selected Poems* (Sheep Meadow Press, 1997) and *J'accuse* (New Directions, 2003), which received the PEN Prize for Poetry in Translation.

PETER COLE is the author of three books of poems, most recently *Things on Which I've Stumbled* (New Directions). His many volumes of translations from Hebrew and Arabic include *The Dream of the Poem: Hebrew Poetry from Muslim and Christian Spain, 950–1492* (Princeton, 2006) and *Curriculum Vitae* by Yoel Hoffmann (New Directions, 2009). Cole has received numerous honors for his work, including the American Academy of Arts and Letters Award in Literature and fellowships from the NEA, the NEH, and the John Simon Guggenheim Foundation. He was named a MacArthur Fellow in 2007.